AMERICAN
FOOTBALL
LINGO

A MINI DICTIONARY
OF
FOOTBALL TERMS

KICK OFF!

1ST AND 10

The first chance or "down" that a team has to move the ball 10 yards. The team is at the beginning of play.

AFC

American Football Conference

AMERICAN FOOTBALL CONFERENCE

A conference name in the NFL.

ATH

Athlete

Used in college football when a player's official position has yet to be determined.

ATT

Attempts

It can refer to either rushing attempts or passing attempts.

AUDIBLE

Changing the play or disguising a call to take advantage of the defense.

BACKS

Players which stand behind the line of scrimmage.

BACK-UP

A reserve player.

BALL HAWK

Someone very skilled in tracking and intercepting the ball.

BLACK MONDAY

The Monday following the last regular season game of the year where coaches' jobs are on the line.

BLITZ

A type of defensive play that involves rushing extra players to try to sack the quarterback.

BLOCK

To prevent a defensive player from getting to the ball-carrier.

BLUE FLAG

The weighted bean bag is used to indicate the place that a key event took place. For example marking the site of a fumble.

BOMB

A long pass.

BOOTLEG

When a quarterback fakes a handoff to a running back and takes it outside either to pass it or run it himself.

BULL RUSH

A defensive player attempting to run through an offensive player rather than trying to make a move to get around him.

BYE

A term used for a week during the season where a team doesn't play.

CB

Cornerback

CHAINS

The ten-yard marker used to
determine if there was a first down.

CHIP SHOT

A short field goal.

CLIPPING

A foul called when a player makes contact with an opponent below the waist from behind.

CORNERBACK

One of the key members of a team's defense. A cornerback is tasked with defending the opposing team's wide receivers and other pass catchers.

D I

Division One

DB

Defensive Back

DBU

Defensive Back University

DE

Defensive End

DEFENSIVE BACK

A term for a team's safeties, cornerbacks, and all defensive players that play further away from the line of scrimmage.

DEFENSIVE BACK UNIVERSITY

Slang term for schools that have a reputation for producing NFL-quality defensive backs.

DEDENSIVE END

The players that line up on the ends of the defensive line.

DEFENSIVE LINE

The team that doesn't have the
ball. The defensive line matches up
against the opposition's offensive
line and consists of a combination
of 3-4 defensive tackles and
defensive ends. A crucial part of a
team's defense.

DEFER

One of the possible choices for the team that wins the coin toss at the start of the game. If a team defers then they get to choose whether to kick or receive at the start of the second half.

DIME BACK

A 6th defensive back.

DIVISION ONE

The highest level of American college athletics. Sometimes abbreviated as D-1.

DL

Defensive line

DOWN

A single play, with teams given 4 downs to make a first down.

DOWN BY CONTACT

In the NFL, when an offensive player is down and touched, he cannot continue the play.

DROP KICK

A kick where the ball is dropped on the ground and kicked after it bounces once.

DUAL-THREAT QUARTERBACK

A quarterback who has a great ability to run and throw the ball.

ELIGIBLE RECEIVER

All players who are able to touch a forward pass.

ENCROACHMENT

A foul that is called whenever a defensive player crosses the line of scrimmage before the ball is snapped.

EXTRA POINT

After scoring a touchdown, a team can choose to attempt a kick equivalent to a 33-year field goal, through the goalposts at each end of the field to earn one additional point.

FALSE START

When an offensive player moves before the snap.

FB

Fullback.

FBS

Football Bowl Subdivision

FF

Forced Fumble

FLAG

The yellow penalty flag that referees throw when a foul has been committed.

FOOTBALL BOWL SUBDIVISION

A collection of NCAA Division 1-A football teams that are eligible for the playoffs and major bowls at the end of the season.

FORCED FUMBLE

A defensive statistic that is awarded when a player causes a ballhandler to lose control of the ball. It does not matter if the ball is recovered or not, simply that a defender caused the ball to come loose.

FREE SAFETY

A member of the team's defensive backfield that guards an opposing team's quarterback.

FS

Free Safety

FULLBACK

A position in the offensive backfield.

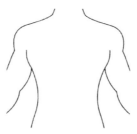

G.O.A.T.

An acronym for "Greatest Of All Time" in reference to a player or team.

GOAT

A slang term that refers to the player that takes the blame for a team's loss.

GRIDIRON

The field of play.

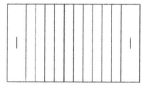

HAIL MARY

A long pass made in desperate situations often at the end in a final attempt to win or tie the game.

HALFBACK

A running back with the main role of running the ball during play when it is handed to them.

HB

Halfback.

HE CAN MAKE ALL THE THROWS

A quarterback who has the ability to complete a high percentage of difficult passes.

HOLDING

A common penalty in the game. It can be called on either an offensive or defensive player any time they try to restrain an opposing player from behind.

HORSE COLLAR TACKLE

When a player is tackled by their neck from behind.

HUDDLE

Players gathered together on the pitch talking tactics as discreetly as possible.

ICING

The practice of the opposing team calling a timeout before an important field goal is kicked.

INJURED RESERVE

A designation that removes an injured player from a team's active roster without cutting them from the team entirely. Only one player who is placed on the IR during the season is allowed to return.

IR

Injured Reserve

KICK OFF SPECIALIST

The player that is tasked with kicking off.

KOS

Kickoff Specialist

LATE HIT

When a player hits another player after the play is considered to be over.

LB

Linebacker

LINEBACKER

A member of a team's defense that plays just behind the defensive line and is used for defending both the pass and the run, as well as rushing the quarterback.

LINE OF SCRIMMAGE

The imaginary line where the football last touched the ground. Neither team can cross the line until the next play has started.

LIVE BALL

A ball that is still considered in-play.

LOCKER ROOM GUY

A player who is great in motivating his team.

LOLB

Left Outside Linebacker

LONG SNAPPER

A member of the special teams unit that is used for snapping the football to the kicker.

LS

Long Snapper

MIDDLE LINEBACKER

A member of a team's defense that lines up in the center of the field just behind the defensive line.

MIKE

A Middle Linebacker.

MLB

Middle Linebacker

MONEYLINE

The bet placed on the team that is favored to win by picking the winning team.

NATIONAL FOOTBALL LEAGUE

The top league in American Football.

NEUTRAL ZONE

The area between the line of scrimmage.

NFC

National Football Conference

NFL

National Football League

NFL GAME PASS

A streaming service that broadcasts every pre-season game live as well as access to replay regular games.

NICKEL BACK

A 5th defensive back.

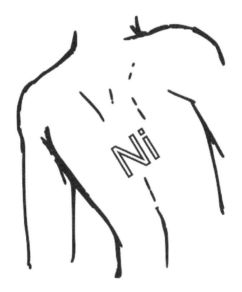

OFFENSIVE LINE

The team that plays when it has the ball.

OFFENSIVE TACKLE

A position on the offensive line.

OFFSIDE

A violation that occurs when a player crosses the line of scrimmage before the ball is snapped.

OLB

Outside Linebacker

OMAHA

A term used by some quarterbacks when calling audibles at the line of scrimmage.

ONSIDE KICK

A move by the kickoff team to retain possession of the football.

ORGANIZED TEAM ACTIVITY

A voluntary session that teams schedule during the off-season. Often in a player's contract, it specifies what activities a players and management can participate in.

OT

Offensive tackle

OT

Over Time

OTA

Organized Team Activity

OUTSIDE LINEBACKER

A defensive position that lines up behind the defensive line and to either side of the middle linebackers.

OVER/UNDER

A gambling term used when betting on the total score of the game. Gamblers can wager on either the "over" (combined score of both teams will be higher than the over/under) or the "under" (combined score will be lower).

OVER TIME

The extra period that's played if the score of a game is tied at the end of regular time.

PA

Points Allowed

PASS BREAK UP

A defensive measure for passes that a player tips or knocks down but does not intercept.

PASS DEFENDED

Same as Pass Deflected. A defensive statistic that is awarded when a player breaks up a passing play without intercepting the pass.

PASS DEFLECTED

Same as Pass Defended. A defensive statistic that is awarded when a player breaks up a passing play without intercepting the pass.

PAT

Point After Touchdown

PBU

Pass Break Up

PD

Pass Defended / Pass Deflected

PERSONAL SEAT LICENSE

A reservation for specific seats that some teams offer to their season ticket holders.

PF

Points For

PHYSICALLY UNABLE TO PERFORM

A list for injured players that may be returned to the active roster within 21 days. If they stay on the list beyond that, they become ineligible to return to play for the rest of the season.

PICK

An interception.

PICK SIX

Slang term used when a defensive player intercepts a pass and returns it for a touchdown for 6 points.

PIG SKIN

The actual football, so called as it used to be made with inflated pig bladders.

PLACE KICK

A kick where the ball is placed still on the ground.

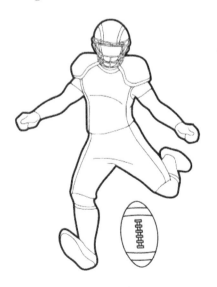

PLAY ACTION

A type of offensive play that involves a fake handoff to a running back in an attempt to draw the defense's attention, followed by a pass to one of the team's receivers.

POCKET

The area that is formed around the quarterback by the offensive line to prevent a defensive player from sacking him.

POCKET

The area between the tackles on the offensive part of the field.

POINTS AFTER TOUCHDOWN

The technical designation for the extra point kicked after a team scores a touchdown.

POINTS ALLOWED

How many points a team's defense has given up over the course of the season.

POINTS FOR

How many points a team has scored over the course of a season.

POOCH

A play from a kickoff where the kicker intentionally kicks the downfield before it spikes into the ground, making it difficult for the returner to handle.

PR

Punt Returner

PSL

Personal Seat License

PUNT RETURNER

A position which is tasked with catching the punts from the opposing team.

PUP

A list for injured players that may be returned to the active roster within 21 days. If they stay on the list beyond that, they become ineligible to return to play for the rest of the season.

QBR

Quarterback Rating

QUARTER

15 minutes of football. Each football game has 4 quarters.

QUARTERBACK

The offensive player responsible for starting play and throwing the ball.

QUARTERBACK RATING

A measure between 0 and 158.3 of the performance of quarterbacks.

RB

Running Back

RED ZONE

The final 20 yards before a team's end zone that is used to indicate that a team is within potential scoring position.

REDSHIRT

It means that a player is not being used one season in order to preserve a year of their eligibility.

REDSHIRT FRESHMAN

Someone who is in their second academic year but their first year of athletic competition.

ROLB

Right Outside Linebacker

ROTATION NUMBER

Each game is given a number. Most ticket operators expect you to give them this number instead of naming a team.

ROVER

A defensive player who specializes in guarding the offensive team's best player.

RPO

Run/Pass Option

RUN INTERFERENCE

To protect the player with the ball from the other team's defensive players.

RUNNING BACK

A player that rushes the ball forward after receiving it from the quarterback.

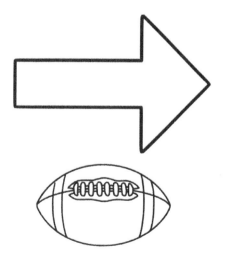

RUN/PASS OPTION

A quarterback's decision making power in the moment to throw the football or run with it.

RZ

Red Zone

SACK

When a quarterback gets tackled behind the line of scrimmage.

SAFETY

An offensive player getting tackled
in their team's end zone where the
defensive team is awarded two
points and given control of the ball.

SAFETY

The safety defensive position, a
member of a team's defensive
backfield.

SAM

Strong side linebacker.

SCOOP-AND-SCORE

When a player picks up a live ball and runs it in for a touchdown.

SCRAMBLE

When a quarterback moves around to avoid the pass rush. An improvised and unplanned move to avoid a sack.

SECONDARY

A term for a team's defensive backfield. It includes a team's safeties and cornerbacks. Their main task is with defending against passing plays.

SECONDARY

The last line of defense is known as the defensive backfield that protect against the pass.

SHOTGUN

A type of offensive formation that has the quarterback receive the snap from several yards behind the line of scrimmage instead of directly from the center at the line.

SIDELINE

The area to stand for team
members who aren't playing.

SLOBBERKNOCKER

A violent collision between two
players.

SPEARING

A dangerous and illegal tackling technique where the tackler leads with the crown of their helmet with their bodyweight powering them forward.

SPOT

Where a ball is marked on the field by the officials.

SPREAD

Offensive formation that lines up the offensive players as wide as possible across the field. These offenses usually start with the quarterback in the shotgun position and use a few wide receivers who are arranged sideline-to-sideline in order to stretch

SQUIB KICK

A low-kicked ball on a kickoff used to limit the other team's ability to make a good return.

SS

Strong Safety

STARING DOWN A RECEIVER

Quarterback who keeps looking at a specific pass catcher, telegraphing where he wants to go with the ball.

STIFF ARM

The arm a player is not using to carry the ball to fend off defenders.

STRAIGHT ARM

The arm a player not using to carry the ball to fend off defenders.

STRONG SAFETY

A member of the defensive backfield that plays deeper than a team's linebackers but not as deep as a free safety or cornerback. They're used to defend against both the pass and the run as necessary.

SUPER BOWL

The biggest football game of the year which is the championship game between the winners of the conferences of the NFL.

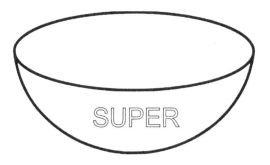

TACKLES FOR LOSS

A tackle made behind the line of scrimmage.

TAKING A KNEE

When a quarterback kneels in order to intentionally down the football as a tactic to run out the clock.

TE

Tight End

TELEGRAPHING

When a quarterback gives away who he's going throw to.

TFL

Tackles for Loss

TIGHT END

A position used for both blocking on the offensive line and as a receiver.

TIP

When a pass is touched

TOUCHDOWN

When a football team moves the ball into the opponent's end-zone to score 6 points.

TRENCHES

The line of scrimmage where the offensive and defensive linemen battle at the snap of the ball where most of the blocking takes place.

TRUE FRESHMAN

A college athlete that did not redshirt for a year but instead played in their first season of eligibility.

TURNOVER

When a defensive player gains possession of the ball after the offensive team loses it.

WEAK-SIDE

The side of the offensive line that has the fewest players.

WIDE RECEIVER

An offensive position dedicated to receiving passes from the quarterback.

WILDCARD

The lower-seeded teams in the NFL playoffs. The four division-winning teams of each conference make up the top four seeds in the playoff bracket, followed by the two wild card teams, which are the teams with the next-best overall records in the conference

WILL

Weak side linebacker.

WISHBONE

An offensive position where a trip of backs shaped like a "Y" are behind the quarterback.

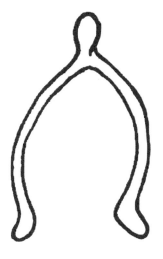

WR

Wide Receiver

YAC

Yards After Catch

THE CONCLUSION

Made in the USA
Las Vegas, NV
06 September 2024

94896281R00066